This book is presented to:

....

From:

....

On this day:

....

the GRACE guide

Live Your One Beautiful Life

SUSIE DAVIS

Abingdon Press

NASHVILLE

THE GRACE GUIDE

LIVE YOUR ONE BEAUTIFUL LIFE

Copyright © 2019 by Susie Davis

All rights reserved.

ISBN 978-1-5018-9842-6

Interior design by Joy O'Meara

19 20 21 22 23 24 25 26 27—10 9 8 7 6 5 4 3 2 1

MANUFACTURED IN THE PEOPLE'S REPUBLIC OF CHINA

For Emily and Sara

who reminded me what
it feels like to be free.

Contents

the
GRACE
guide

Introduction

This is a book about you.

I want you to know you. I want to hear your story—and for you to tell it to yourself again. Because inside your story, there is God-sized wonder. Inside your story, there is awe.

The kind of awe you feel when you look up at the big blue Texas sky. Or when you see the Colorado mountains standing sturdy and strong, sentinels to the glory of creation. The thing is, the grandeur you see in nature isn't just external—it is internal, too. It's tucked deep in your narrative.

Outside, I see God's creativity and care everywhere

in nature. Inside your story, we'll see his creativity and care, too.

This book is a guide to help you understand and celebrate your unique story. Inside your own narrative, you'll find discoveries big and small that point to the God who loves you.

I'd like to start with a small story of my own that often reminds me of how God shows his love.

Twice a year, my daughters and I make a trip to Round Top, Texas, to see the largest antique show in the state. We shop and play and spend some good time together.

A couple years back, our trip together was over my birthday. To celebrate, my oldest daughter, Emily, surprised me with something special and amazing: she made flower crowns out of delicate pink and white roses for me and her younger sister to wear. It was delightful. In the moment, I was giddy. The gesture was so kind and thoughtful and whimsical. It was the first time I can remember ever wearing a flower crown.

When we left the country cottage where we were staying to go shopping, I suddenly felt self-conscious as a fifty-year-old woman walking around with a flower crown on her head. Certainly, I've seen women wearing them before but usually only at weddings or in fairytale picture books for children. But every time I started to feel awkward, I would just look over at my daughters and see them laughing, smiling, and happy. When I looked at them, so free in their joy, I would toss off the self-consciousness and sink into my own wonder.

The flower crown made me feel loved and free in the face of shyness, self-doubt, and preconceived ideas about who I was supposed to be. Who the world tells me I'm supposed to be. And the flower crown became an emblem of grace for me: an unexpected gift that let me live more freely.

In your life and mine, God offers grace. It's all ours. But until we put it on and actually walk around in it, we don't experience the freedom.

As you are reading this book, and uncovering your story, you will be reminded that you are a **dearly loved daughter of God.**

His love for you started even before you were born, and his love follows you everywhere. You will see his hand of blessing all over your story and, I hope, wear that blessing like a crown of flowers upon your head.*

---

* Psalm 138:5 NLT

CHAPTER ONE

God's Grace for You

He converses and delights Himself with me
incessantly, in a thousand and a thousand ways,
and treats me in all respects as His favorite.

—BROTHER LAWRENCE

In a small vintage suitcase on the top shelf of my closet sits a treasure trove of handwritten letters. Some are love notes from my husband penned thirty years ago, back when we were dating. Others—irregular shaped pages ripped from spiral notebooks covered in crayon marks and unsteady penmanship—are from my children when they were young. Of course, I have dozens of notes and letters from both my mom and my dad over the years. And then a few saved from my grandmother, mostly birthday cards when I was little. I love seeing her long slender lettering, ever always signing "Lovingly, Grandma."

I keep old letters. And I read them when the world knocks my heart around. They center me. They remind me of the important things and the beautiful things. And more than anything, they remind me I am deeply loved. I am grateful that the people in my life took time to write me letters, because it's tangible evidence that I matter to them.

God writes us letters, too. He doesn't slip them in the little suitcase at the top of the closet. He doesn't leave them in the mailbox to be discovered at the end of a long day. He leaves them outside all over creation and inside sprinkled into the details of our daily lives.

I am wondering … do you recognize the love notes he leaves in your life?

When I look back over mine, I see his love and care in my story everywhere. There is one incredible story with God and me concerning a tree my dad planted on the grounds of my junior high school. Another in the thoughtfulness of an older woman who invited me to her Bible study that eventually resulted in God starting a huge healing process in my life. I can look back and remember God's kindness to me when, as a young mother in a new city, the ladies in my new neighborhood included me in their book club. In each of these instances, I felt seen, cared for, and loved.

I see his love in the way he answers my prayers. And how, even when I am by myself, I never feel alone. I look back over my life and see that it's even in the way God brings little things into my life to delight me, like the yellow finches I see at the bird feeder outside my window right now. In all my life, God pads my path with little love notes, spreading his love and light through everything everywhere.

Over the years, I have come to understand that I am a well-loved child. The center of God's focus. Someone he longs to care for, communicate with, shower his love on. And you know what? You are, too.

Inside the Bible there are all kinds of personal love letters to you and me from God. Inside those pages, there are all sorts of truths meant to bring us closer to who God is and how he feels about us. One of the most beautiful little love notes is tucked in the Gospel of John.

It says,

> *But to all who believed him and accepted him, he*
> *gave the right to become children of God.*[*]

Do you think of yourself as his child, his daughter? Because I sure do. And what's written there for me is also true for you. When you believe God is who he says he is and then you accept his gift of love through Jesus, you become a dearly loved daughter. Isn't that incredible?

All those years ago when I accepted God's invitation to trust him, I became his daughter so that means I am in his family. And that decision was the best decision I've ever made in my whole life. Because it's impacted every single aspect of my life.

My relationship with God made a huge impact on who I chose to marry. It impacted how my husband, Will, and I raised our children. It made a big difference in the vocation I chose. And the decision to become a daughter is why I'm even writing this to you now.

---

[*] John 1:12 NLT

What if God could write you a letter right now? What do you think he would say to you?

I imagine if he could write you a note right now, here's what he would say:

Dear Daughter,

I love you. I've always loved you. And you need to know, I will never leave you. I will never abandon you. Others may come and go, but I will always stay. There is nothing you could do to undo my love for you. There is nothing you could say to drive me away. You are my daughter, and I delight in you. More than anything, I'd love to talk with you. I want you to include me in your day. But even if you don't, I'm leaving signs all over creation to remind you of how much I love you. I'm orchestrating the tiniest details in your life to show my affection ... because I'm always right there. Loving you, watching out for you, and taking care of you.

Love, God

Do you believe it? Can you embrace it? I pray so. Because when you do, that's when you'll see how you

When you
believe God
is who
he says he
is and then you
accept his gift
of love through Jesus,
you become a dearly
loved daughter.

are the recipient of the best and biggest love ever: God's love. And you'll see how his love for you overshadows and showers your entire life with blessing.

You'll be able to look back on your life and see all the love letters. Far too many to fit in a little suitcase at the top of your closet. You are deeply loved by the God of all creation. He offers grace and kindness to you. My prayer is that you also offer that grace and kindness to yourself.

CHAPTER TWO

Grace

Invitation

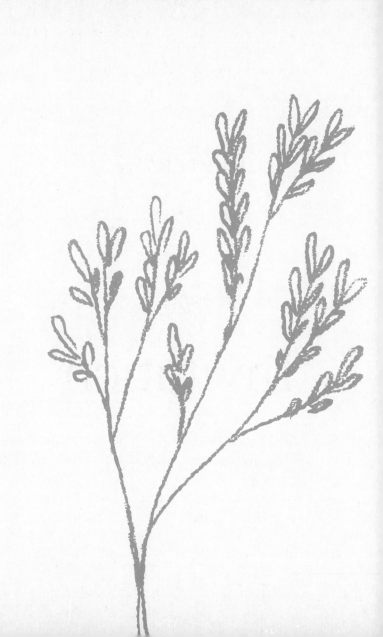

Our hearts are made for you, O Lord,
and they will not find rest until they rest in you.

—AUGUSTINE

Summer is here. I know because last night the fireflies made their appearance for the first time. They took turns bumping gently against the family room windows, tiny lights flickering off and on against the dark sky. Their light so small, yet, against the sleepy night sky, they shone bright.

Some people are like that, too. Their story bumps into yours, and for a moment you see their light, brilliant and bright, against the everyday world revealing something eternal. You see the love of God in their lives.

The first time I remember seeing God's light in a person's life that helped me understand the eternal was at church. Yep, my first impression of God was when I heard Dr. Howland preach at University Christian Church here in Austin. University Christian Church is a gorgeous old English-Gothic style building with a tall steeple. Inside the sanctuary are big stained-glass windows with wooden floors and pews. I don't remember what Dr. Howland said when he stood up front because I was only five or six years old. But I do remember his voice was deep and gentle. And that he wore a black robe and shiny black shoes.

After church he would greet my parents out front by the big wooden doors, me included. And I would have to say equally impressive to me was Mr. Jackson, an elderly man, who stood outside after Sunday school under the portico and handed out M&Ms to the children. Another friendly face of God. I'm grateful for them both. These people made me feel seen and valued. Adults who took time in their busy schedules to pause and acknowledge me.

What about you? What was your first impression of God? Was it good or bad? Do you remember how old you were? Or where you were or what happened in that place? Think back to that time and maybe write something down about that initial meeting. It doesn't need to be anything too descriptive or long or complicated. Just the first thing that comes to mind.

Okay then, what happened after that? How did that initial impression lead you to a correct or incorrect picture of who God is?

My first impression led me to a belief that God was friendly and approachable ... and that maybe he gave out chocolate candies. That he was distinctly masculine. Gentle and polite. Whereas a reader, Patti, wrote to me telling that her first impression of God was that he was egotistical. Now, she says, she really has gotten to know him, and she sees he's full of mercy and grace. For Patti, it took trusting God to understand his goodness. I sometimes like to lean into that first impression of God—to remember him as a gentle giver of little gifts. Maybe you're like me. Or maybe you're like Patti, and you have to remind yourself to turn to your new understanding of God, and away from the old.

Inside and out—
and all about
my life—there is God.
His grace floods
over me.
Love scattered
across all the days and
weeks and years.

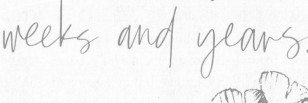

How was your path to God lined with either a good or bad first impression? For so many women I know, their impression of God was built around their fathers. And sadly for many, that was a negative impression that led to further difficulties in understanding that God the Father is unconditionally loving and tender, full of grace.

Or I am thinking of another dear daughter whose grandmother was a strong matriarchal influence in her family who honored God and served him but didn't know his grace. She controlled the family with all kinds of her spiritual rules, like how long to read the Bible and what kinds of clothes women should wear. She often verbally berated the rule-breakers and, as a result, the grandmother entangled her granddaughter in all kinds of legalistic thinking.

I want you to think about your spiritual history because it affects where are you in your relationship with God right now and how you relate to him. It impacts your ability to receive all the grace he has for you. And it might be why you don't feel close to him now.

Since the first impression I had of God was that he was friendly and approachable, my decision to follow

Jesus wasn't a difficult one. When, seven years later, a college-aged Young Life leader named Kenny shared the gospel with me, I prayed to God, asking him to be involved in my everyday life. That's when I trusted my life to him. That's when I became a Christian.

While these men are not God, the good aspects of those men were images of God's goodness to me. And the kindness they showed me are like little lights in a dark world, leading me down a path to find God. Their lives entwined in mine as I caught a bigger picture of God's character.

Who are the people who delivered the good news in your life about God's love and grace? And in what ways did they lead you to truth or mistruth about God's true character? In what ways did they represent a clear or muddied picture of how God feels about you? How you came to know about God impacts how you feel about him. The people who led you to God are a part of your spiritual heritage.

Looking back over my life now, I can see how God is not Mr. Jackson handing out M&Ms under the portico, and he's not Dr. Howland in a black robe and shiny black shoes preaching while I sit on a wooden pew; but he is Immanuel, which means "God with me."[*] In the best and most beautiful times of my life, God was there with me. In the most awful and gut-wrenching times, God was right beside me. Inside and out—and all about my life—there is God. His grace floods over me. Love scattered across all the days and weeks and years.

I want you to have that kind of grace. The kind of grace you know deep in your bones, but you also live out in your everyday life. That deep grace of God starts in the smallest places. For me it was a single prayer of invitation, asking God into my life and allowing him access to all of it. I never could have believed that little prayer would change so much for me. If I could, I would thank my twelve-year-old self. I'd say:

Oh Susie, thank you. Though when you wake up tomorrow, you won't feel any different than you do today, the prayer you prayed to receive Jesus in your life changes everything for the rest of your life. You've been invited into something beautiful and magnificent that you didn't earn, and you don't deserve … but it's all yours. And that will always be true. I'm so grateful you made this

---

[*] Matthew 1:23

decision because you're going to need all the faith you can get in the next couple years. It's going to be rough, and you will suffer greatly. But God will be right there with you, Immanuel, in the most personal ways. He will be closer than your best friend. Closer than your mother and father. He will be your protector, your comfort, and your guide. And his love will be your light in some dark days. I just want you to know how very proud I am of you. And that I love you.

What about you? Have you made that kind of decision? Where is the light in your life? Inside these pages, I'm going to ask a lot of questions and I'm going to write some letters to help you think through your one beautiful life with God. I hope that you'll find your story in my story. My prayer is that you'll awaken to the enormity of God's love and grace by experiencing it in a new way. A deeper way that will enable you to live with joy and freedom.

CHAPTER THREE

Grace for Yesterday

Grace … connects us to the invisible One in an eternal love relationship that fills us with joy we have never known before and gives us rest of heart that we would have thought impossible.

—DAVID PAUL TRIPP

Texans love talking about the weather. You can go anywhere in the state and strike up a friendly conversation about what's going on outside. My husband, in particular, loves getting up and giving amateur meteorological updates. He wakes every morning, looks out the window at the expanse of sky behind our house, and then checks the weather report online. "It's gonna rain today.

We're going to get some more water in the creek." I like it when it rains. That just means it's time to wear rain boots, of which I have quite the collection. But mostly, in this month of July, Will peers out the window and says, "Hot and dry this week. We're getting upward toward one hundred degrees." In which case I know at some point in the afternoon, I'll take a much-needed dip in the pool. Because of Will's morning weather updates, I usually have a good idea what's headed my way for the upcoming week.

Of course, that's not the way it works in our personal lives. You can't always anticipate or prepare for things the way we do with the weather. I mean sure, we write things down in our calendars and plan on making it to meetings and appointments. But no matter what's written down, things come up unexpectedly. We're just going along in our one life and then boom—something surprising happens. Smaller things like canceled dinner plans, an unexpected expense, a hurtful phone call. Or maybe something hits hard. A car wreck, a cancer diagnosis, some inexplicable tragedy in the lives of our family or friends.

Everyone experiences those kinds of unwanted surprises that leave us in gulfs of great sadness. They're unavoidable. And that kind of heartbreak will hit you whether you live a careful life or a careless one. All of us, at some point in time, are surprised by the suffering. Every single one of us.

One of the most significant points of suffering happened to me when I was fourteen years old. I witnessed the murder of my teacher. A fellow classmate walked into my eighth-grade classroom with a rifle and shot our teacher. In the aftermath of that tragedy, I loved God, but I didn't trust him. I felt God must have been too busy on the other side of the world to notice my situation and take care of me.

That pain point in my life brought all kinds of misinformation about God and it impacted our relationship for a very long time. Looking back now, I see how I was disappointed in God after the murder took place. I started thinking of God as distant and unemotional. Because what kind of a good Father lets his daughter experience that kind of suffering? I still prayed to him like crazy, but I didn't expect protection. And so I started trying to take care of myself, which resulted in all kinds of unhealthy anxiety and hyper-control issues.

When bad things happen in life, we often unintentionally embrace a warped perception of God and some unhealthy behaviors along with it. I sure did. Maybe you too? Think back over your life and make a short list of some hurtful things that have happened to you. As best you remember, describe one of your most significant personal pain points. Maybe your dad left your family. Or your best friend betrayed you. Or perhaps you had some personal failure you just can't seem to shake. When did it happen? Where did it happen? Was it sudden and violent or did it creep in day after day? Take a minute and write it down.

Now, try to evaluate how that situation impacted you. Did you keep loving God but distrust him like I did? Or did you reject him altogether, believing he was unjust or maybe even nonexistent?

After you take a minute with that, answer this question with some prayerful introspection: What did you lose during that time? For me, I lost my sense of safety at home (the boy who killed my teacher lived three doors up from me), in my school, and in the community at large. I lost my childlike innocence, and, in some sense, I lost a huge part of my childhood because of the graphic fears that constantly filled my mind. And then finally, for a long while, I lost the idea of God as a caring Father. What about you? How was your story altered because of suffering?

For one dear daughter I mentor, she still grieves the death of her dad when she was fourteen years old. Another still deals with the fact that her mother verbally abused her all her life. Another struggles to heal over a sexual assault that happened in her early twenties. And still another is walking out the new revelation that her husband had multiple affairs. Walking alongside these women in the middle of their suffering and grief is humbling and a constant reminder that suffering and grief are a part of all our lives.

God never promised a life without pain and suffering. He actually gives us a forecast about the reality of pain in our lives. It's an honest one that we don't like. Here's what Jesus said: "Here on earth you will have many trials and sorrows."*

---

*   John 16:33 NLT

*Embrace
and celebrate*
the days when the
sun is shining
and it's perfectly
wonderful outside.
Don't sit inside terrified,
just waiting for
the next natural disaster.

There it is, and yet often, we act stunned and offended when suffering comes. We act as if God lied to us and betrayed us. I know I did. But God didn't lie. There will be trials. There will be hardship. There will be suffering. In your life and mine.

I've had my share, but I'm sure to have more. You probably will, too. That statement is not meant to scare you; it is meant to free you to live your one beautiful life with God today. Embrace and celebrate the days when the sun is shining and it's perfectly wonderful outside. Don't sit inside terrified, just waiting for the next natural disaster. Yes, bad things happen but that's true regardless whether you live a carefree life or try to control every aspect—so what's the point of doing the latter? You have to get out there and live your one beautiful life.

And then, when the storms come, know that God is close whether you feel his presence or not. And hold on to the fact that God promises not just to be with us but to also bring something beautiful in the broken places. Yes, even in the hardest situations, somehow God makes things beautiful.

If you find yourself in the middle of a dark or confusing time and you wonder if God even cares about you, I have good news: God is not finished writing your story. It's not over yet. As long as you're still breathing, you can know with all certainty that God's not done yet.

If I could go back in time and forecast something for myself, here's what I would do. I would fiercely hug my fourteen-year-old self on that day so long ago, and then I would sit with her while she cried. After that, when the questions surfaced about why God allowed such a horror, I would say:

Honestly, Susie, this day is the worst. It is brutal and awful and so very sad. And I think you already know this, but what happened here is something you'll never forget. It will impact you for the rest of your life. But I need you to know something very important in the middle of this chaos: You will not always feel afraid and sad. And God did not forsake you. He never left you. And he never will. *I know it feels like he did, and it looks like he did, but he didn't.* It will take years for you to actually know and embrace that as truth, but it will stand true. Most important, God will take all that happened today, every single piece of it, and he will over-redeem it in your life. And unbelievable as it sounds, he will comfort and cover you with the most creative and beautiful thing you've ever seen. What you see that day will be one of the most amazing things you'll ever experience—and it will just be between you and God. You will know exactly what it means when he says he'll make beauty out of ashes. Inside that beauty, you will be healed. Truly, deeply healed. You'll know the love of God in a new way. It will be even more significant for you than that first decision you made to trust him. So Susie, hold on to hope. Even if it's just a tiny flicker of a flame. Because I'm sitting here next to you telling you the truth: God is present. And he will restore you.

That's what I wish I could tell my fourteen-year-old self. And I would also mention that at fifty-five years old, she should expect frequent joy overloads at even the smallest things. I would tell her that what she loses at fourteen years old, she gains back in the coming years and, by the time she's fifty, her joy will overwhelm her daily.

I would tell her the source of her inexpressible joy is Jesus.[*] And that close to him is where grace lives glad, regardless of circumstances.

---

[*]   1 Peter 1:18

CHAPTER FOUR

Grace for
Today

Genuine self-knowledge begins by looking at God and noticing how God is looking at us. Grounding our knowing of our self in God's knowing anchors us in reality. It also anchors us in God.

—DAVID BRENNER

When my husband's parents died, we ended up with quite a few of their belongings. The dining room table, a beautiful chandelier, and a small painted French dresser among other treasures. While emptying the contents of their home, we also found lots of old photos from Will's childhood. I loved seeing all those pictures, but Will did not. He said his baby pictures reminded him of a time when he was young and awkward. As a child, Will wore corrective shoes because he was pigeon-toed and he also struggled greatly with eye-hand coordination. For me, knowing those things about him when he was young only endears him more to me. But even that doesn't make him friendlier toward those photos from his youth. He is the only person I know who truly doesn't like his baby pictures. He actually said that he wanted to throw them away, but I didn't let him. I tucked them away, out of his sight, and am hopeful one day he'll grow to appreciate them.

I'm pretty fanatical about people loving their baby selves. I wrote a whole chapter about it in *Dear Daughters: Love Letters to the Next Generation*. Because I think it's incredibly important that you love yourself—past, present, future. And that includes your precious, tiny baby self. How do you feel about your baby pictures when you see them? Do they make you smile, or do you wish you could throw them away like Will does? It's an interesting thing to think about, isn't it? That something as simple as how seeing yourself at a different age of your life informs you about how you feel about yourself today.

I'd be interested to sit down with you and a big ole photo album of yours from when you were growing up, or to look through your old junior high and high school yearbooks. I'd love to hear the stories that accompany the photos and to watch you revisit your past, to have you recall your story. It would tell me so much about your life, how you became you, and what you think about that process. It would also tell me a lot about what you think about yourself now: the combination of all those happy, sad, embarrassing parts of you from all those photos.

Along those lines, can we do something really quick? I'd love for you to take a minute and list out ten adjectives that describe you. Just quickly jot down ten words that best describe you. Now look over that list. Of course, some not-so-happy words will probably come up, but I'm hopeful that at least half of those descriptors were positive.

After writing out that list, I want you to give your list an honest assessment. What does it say about how you feel about you? Though you might think this is grossly introspective, the truth is that you think thoughts about yourself all the time. And for most women I talk with, those thoughts are usually pretty negative. Self-talk like, "I'm so fat" or "She's so much smarter than me" or "No one really cares about me." Statements like that and much worse swirl in the minds of so many women.

The thing is, much of how you feel about yourself today is informed by how you feel about yourself over the years you've been you. So it started back with all those pictures of yourself: who you were in them, and what you think of that person now. The memories you have of yourself are carried forward, telling you who you are today.

Now, ready for the next assignment? List ten ways God describes you. Yep. Don't put a ton of thought into it, just write down ten ways God thinks of you. Afterward, check to see if there are stark discrepancies between your list and God's list.

When I had women go through this exercise in my mentorship program, they often had a lot of negative descriptors on both lists. It broke my heart. Because what you think about how God feels for you determines most of how you think about yourself. If you believe God made you distinct, original, and beautiful, but you don't think he feels all love and grace toward you, then there's a real disconnect.

Jesus said the greatest command was to love God and your neighbor as yourself. Did you catch that part? Love your neighbor *as you love yourself.* God expects you to love yourself. He *wants* that for you. God wants you to love yourself. Wholly, unconditionally, with tender love and grace over all the days of your life. If only you could think of yourself the way God thinks of you, then spread that rich grace over every single day you've been alive. That's how God wants you to love yourself with the same grace he expects you to give to others.

God loves you and he wants you to think of yourself the way he thinks of you. He calls you his dearly loved daughter.[*] He is thinking of you day and night. He cares for you. He has a "passionate absorbed interest"[**] in you.

Oh, and this too … God's not disappointed in you. The only way you could be a disappointment to God is if you surprised him. And you can't surprise God.

---

[*]   1 John 3:1

[**]   Hannah Hurnard, *Kingdom of Love* (Carol Stream, IL: Tyndale House, 1981), 48.

Not with yesterday's screwups or today's missed opportunities. Because nothing in your life surprises him. So you cannot disappoint him. His love for you is unmatched, unaltered, and completely steadfast. A love like no other. A run-to kind of love, not a run-away kind of love.

God knows every single detail about your life. And He loves you.

But do you really believe it?

I want you and God to be close. And I want you to see how his love for you is so creative and personal. I want you to experience the love of God in your life in the deepest way. Because it's inside that relationship that you'll start to love yourself. And there will be an everyday peace and joy in your life that will be a bright light in a dark world.

Imagine this ... what if you got to sit across from your younger self? The younger self who makes you feel uncomfortable because she wasn't quite enough. Because she was pigeon-toed, or she was awkward, or because she was too loud, or too insecure, or too ugly. Not good enough. Imagine that younger self. Say you sat across from her, maybe sharing coffee.

What would you say to encourage her?

What would you want her to know about God and her life?

I know that's a lot to think about. And maybe something you don't want to think about at all. Perhaps there's shame tucked in your past, or maybe regrets about the way things have happened. I know. I have those feelings about my story, too.

But the thing is: How can you love the life you have if you don't have a genuine love for yourself? And have you ever considered this? How can you be a bright light in a dark world if you still think of your own life as dark and unworthy of overwhelming grace? You will live with yourself longer than your mother or father, longer than the person you marry. In and out of all your longest-lasting relationship, there you'll be just you.

And if you don't love—and have grace over—the person you were and are, you will lack the ability to shine

God wants you
to love yourself
with the same
grace he expects
you to give
to others.

bright and to truly enjoy your life and your most important relationships. I want you to love your one beautiful life. The whole of it. Even in the hard places because there is beauty tucked everywhere.

When you look back over your story and give yourself grace, you will actually live a more beautiful life.

You don't have to love the decisions you made or the things that happened to you, but real grace, deep life-changing grace—the kind you walk around in every single day—is about receiving the grace God has for you to love the person you were and are. Because he certainly does.

God loves you past, present, and future. When he invites you into a relationship with him, he already knows every step you take. He knows every decision you'll make. He even knows every little thing you think. And inside all that, there is deep love. Twenty-four hours a day, seven days a week, fifty-two weeks a year, and every single year of your life until you meet him, face-to-face *love*.

Can you even imagine it? That the God of all creation loves you through all your time and space, in the most intimate way? It's true, and if that's not enough, his grace through Jesus covers your life.

And when you truly experience that grace, you'll begin to extend a deep, rich kindness to yourself—a kind of inner hospitality towards yourself.

Grace is inner hospitality.

It's that inner hospitality that can overcome all the negativity, self-loathing, and shame. My end goal for you is that you could look at any picture of yourself from any age and feel tenderness and compassion. That I could point to any picture of you in a yearbook and you would smile and offer a kind word to that girl. Wouldn't that be amazing?

I think the best way to get to this inner hospitality today is to embrace the reality of God's love for you. You can read about it in the Bible, you can listen to your favorite teachers preach on it, but until you get it for yourself, you'll be missing the peace.

So hey, how about this? What if you write a letter from God to you? What do you think God would want to say just to you? Imagine it for a minute. If he could speak directly to you, what would he want you to know, from his heart right to yours? Think as honestly as you can about it. As free of judgment as you know he would be toward you. With as much grace as you can imagine, then write those words. What would God say to you? Write it all down.

CHAPTER FIVE

Grace for Families

We are loved because we are his children,
because we are.

—MADELEINE L'ENGLE

Every summer, we take off for a few days and join my big ole extended family at the Frio River in Leakey, Texas. We've stayed at River Haven annually every August for over twenty years. The Frio trip serves as a holiday marker in my year, much like Christmas. It's the time all the Gerries, the Staffords, and the Davises gather at the river to talk and laugh and play.

Mornings at the Frio are my favorite. I love waking up early and taking my cup of coffee to the big wooden picnic table on the back porch overlooking the river. I like to sit and write a little bit. Then slowly, all the people start waking up. It's usually my sister's grandkids who are up first. They spill out on the porch in their pajamas, ready to eat breakfast and play. Their little voices fill the air, a complement to the river song below.

Later I'll walk cabin to cabin, bumming things I forgot, like butter for my eggs. Everyone leaves their doors unlocked and no matter whose porch you wind up on, it's likely you'll sit to talk for a while. And whether we're up at the cabins or down by the river, we take turns holding babies and playing with the children. We're just one big family and from the outside, it probably looks idyllic.

But we're like any other family. We have our stuff. We've walked through trying times, outside of family and inside of it. And when we come to the Frio, we bring our whole selves. All the memories of the good times and the difficult ones that we've gone through together and alone.

At the Frio, I am distinctly aware of my roles as daughter, sister, aunt, and friend. All those roles combine to make me—the good and bad of me, the right and wrong of me. The way I've succeeded and met expectations, and the way I've failed and missed the mark. I want to be so much for my family, but I'm not always. This big family getaway always reminds me, even calls to me, of my need for grace. I need it. Desperately. From God and from my family.

Maybe you feel the same way when you think of your roles in your family. Perhaps you've disappointed as a daughter. Or you offended your sister or your brother. Or maybe you've been in a position with someone in your family where you've needed to extend grace to a mother, father, sister, or brother. It goes both ways; it's normal to need grace all around. So what does it look like to put yourself in that position—to extend and receive grace in your family?

The first thing that helps is setting perspective. Remembering we all arrive into the world as tiny, dependent babies, aching to have our needs met. And we seek to have our needs met from broken parents. It's in that environment that we grow and develop coping skills. Our parents are the models to sort out the difficulties in the world, and no matter how fantastic your parents are, they taught you some unhealthy coping skills either overtly or by example.

In my family of origin, we call one of those un-healthy patterns "Gerrie guilt." It's this pesky little tendency to overthink things and feel bad about our part in them. Gerrie guilt causes us to wonder too long on what the right thing to do is when a situation is gray. Or whether we have inadvertently hurt someone's feelings. Gerrie guilt could be described as worry. Or fear. There's a strong thread of that kind of anxiety in our family, and you can draw a straight line up through our lineage to my maternal grandmother. She, too, was a worrier.

The problem with Gerrie guilt is that it can make us want to be too careful, too apologetic, too responsible. If we let it overwhelm us, we might even walk on eggshells just to avoid "getting in trouble." And then it folds into people-pleasing, which in turn creates opportunities for inauthenticity. (See? Everybody's family has stuff.)

So as an example, when my Gerrie guilt kicks in, it can make me feel vulnerable and exposed. It can make me want to reach out for a covering of affirmation and the assurance that I'm doing the right thing. Or it can make me reach out for forgiveness even if I have done nothing wrong. If someone looks at me sideways, Gerrie guilt can kick in and then I can obsess on it until it really bothers me. It's false guilt. Like a little personal anxiety attack. And if I don't take this guilt to God and sort it out, I can get really unhealthy. I need grace for my Gerrie guilt.

And guess who else needs grace for that kind of guilt? Oh, about half my family. Yep, it's a strong gene that swallows up a significant number of us. The best thing we've done as a family is talk about it. We name it, we laugh about it, and therein we diminish much of its power. It's a beautiful thing to open up about family weakness.

What about you? Where could you open up about your family of origin's weakness in a way that doesn't push blame but rather exposes a universal fragility and need for grace? Sit prayerfully for a minute on this one. Ask God to show you something you haven't seen in your family.

Who keeps coming to mind? I bet you are thinking of someone in your family who's difficult. Who is that person? What is the main problem? What do you feel needs to happen with them to make things better?

Okay now, you have your mental list. What if I asked

you to tear up that list and let it go? What if this time, instead of thinking about the ways they hurt you or the ways they haven't measured up, you wonder about them a little bit in a more gracious, curious way?

Is there a chance they're trying to get something from you that they didn't get from an important person in their life? Do they want things that seem unreasonable? Or perhaps you're trying to get something from them that you want but can't secure?

I talk with so many dear daughters working through these kinds of things with their families. They have dads they need to extend grace toward or moms they need to receive grace from. And the same thing happens inside sibling relationships. It's messy. Sometimes it's painful. And if you happen to be focusing too much on everyone else's "perfect family," you feel like your family is completely messed up and beyond grace. But that's not true.

If you and the person you consider the most difficult in your family are still here, there's time for God to do something for the two of you. And the bottom-line truth is, if you're reading this now, you need to be the first to step up with a huge, heaping heart full of grace.

A heart like that starts by acknowledging the brokenness in yourself and in others. And it might even mean tearing up that list of things that would fix it all and make it better—and just let it be what it is—even if it looks like it's shattered at your feet. It's inside family that we forget that grace isn't always a *work harder* kind of thing—sometimes it's forgiving and releasing and *being in* what you actually have.

If this sounds overwhelming or if little tears are pricking the corners of your eyes, please take it to a counselor's office and work it out. With or without that problem family member. Yes, it's hard work but it's worth the time, the energy, and the money to repair your heart. And I have to say: There is no greater place for grace to live than inside a family.

And if you don't have time or resources to see a counselor, can I offer a suggestion? Start taking care of your own soul. Offer yourself some mother care that you may be missing. One of the best ways to deal with difficult or unhealthy people—or a family system that continues to rock your world—is by establishing some boundaries.

One dear daughter I mentor told me she was dreading an upcoming family reunion vacation because she

Where could
you open up about your
family of origin's weakness
in a way that doesn't
push blame but rather
exposes a universal
fragility and need
for grace?

has a very stressful relationship with her sister. She felt anxious, bracing against what she knew would be a taxing weeklong trip. All the old patterns, all the old conversations, and all the history was welling up inside of her, making her feel as if she was completely helpless.

So I asked her what was one thing she would really like to do on the trip that would fill her up. Just one little refueling technique that could give her a tiny space for peace in what would be an otherwise demanding week. She thought for a minute and then told me if she could just sneak away for an evening and get down to the beach to get a peek at the stars, she could get through. So I challenged her to a night of beach and stars self-care. After her trip, she told me she snuck away four times that week. I was so happy for her. While we usually can't fix other people, we can fix our response to them.

Here is the real truth: We're all broken from the beginning. And though we'd like to piece together and make our families perfect, that's God's job. So we fall on him, begging for grace for our broken selves and grace for the broken people we come from.

I love what poet Jan Richardson writes regarding brokenness. She says, "Look into the hollows of your hands and ask what wants to be gathered there, what abundance waits among the scraps that come to you, what feast will offer itself from the fragments that remain."*

Herein lies the real feast in family; there are precious fragments that remain. Write a letter to God, thanking him for your family, especially for the ones who need grace.

---

* Jan Richardson, *The Cure for Sorrow* (Orlando: Wanton Gospeller, 2016), 161.

CHAPTER SIX

Grace for Marriage

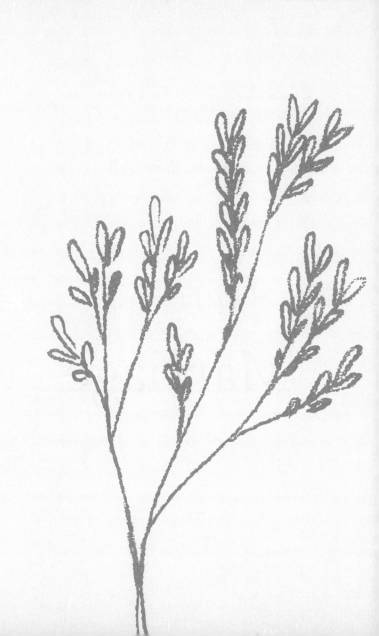

So—you marry a sinner. And you love, accept, and forgive that sinner as you yourself expect to be loved, accepted, and forgiven.

—ELISABETH ELLIOT

It was a quick little trip for Will and me: just three days in Orange County, California, to record a seven-hour video teaching series on marriage. To celebrate finishing the project, we enjoyed dinner at a gorgeous restaurant at Dana Point, overlooking the Pacific Ocean. We ate amazing food, marveled at the view, and chatted about the upcoming marriage series we were planning for our own church. All was well until we got in the car to head back to the hotel. I was relaxing, watching day turn into night, and Will was driving.

Suddenly, I realized Will was off course. I looked over at Will and asked if he knew where he was going. He admitted he somehow missed a turn or something and that he was correcting his route. I straightened up and jumped into action. I thought to myself, "I could easily get us back on course," so I started offering directions. Now, I'm not sure if your husband is like mine, but Will's not the guy who likes a side-seat driver, so when I started pointing the way and telling him where to go, he started getting angry. Suffice it to say in a matter of minutes while lost in L.A., we got in a humongous fight over something as teeny tiny as finding our way back to our hotel. All this, right after seven hours talking about how to do marriage well. And then just five minutes from the time we got lost to the time we lost our temper with each other.

I probably don't need to tell you that there's no relationship that needs grace more than marriage. Take two independently created lives, have a minister marry them until death parts them, and you'll have lots of chances for friction and lots of chances for grace. The fact that God created marriage as a relationship that not only fuses two into one[*] but is also meant to last a lifetime makes for a space in need of an abundance of grace. There is no relationship more intimate and no relationship that requires the rawest authenticity like that in a marriage.

No doubt Will didn't understand the depth of what he'd gotten into when he married me. I was a little blonde girl full of idealistic notions about what marriage looked like. I wanted a Prince Charming, I suppose because I thought of myself as a princess. But Will was no Prince Charming, and I was no princess. While our honeymoon phase lasted a good long time, it was because we both held tight and worked hard. It was only when we found ourselves at the utter end of a try-hard marriage, full of unresolved hurt and unforgiveness, that we had the chance for a grace-filled marriage.

I talk with so many dear daughters in the same space I was in early in my marriage. They are full of expectation based on several different things, but mostly, they picture a marriage contingent on what their hearts feel. Because it's usually feelings that draw

---

[*]   Genesis 2:22–23

us into marriage, and we expect feelings will sustain marriage. But nothing could be further from the truth. A God-honoring marriage is based less on feeling and more on forgiveness. It's based less on your expectations of what you can do and more on utter dependence on what God can do.

Early in my marriage, I had no realistic concept of the deep sacrifice required. Nor did Will. Neither of us had any idea the depth of our own selfishness, our own independence. We had no idea what it looked or felt like for God to meld us into one. But it's when you face what you're actually made of—flaws and all—that you have space for grace.

Looking back now over my nearly thirty-five years of marriage with Will, I can see that's where I've been the messiest, the most unbeautiful, and sometimes the meanest. It's the place I've let all my most desperate feelings find voice in the times I've felt discouraged or defeated. And the same is true of Will. I've witnessed the most glorious and the absolute worst in his life, too. And somewhere in the mix of all, there is God and his extension of supernatural forgiveness in our marriage.

What about you? Think back about how your marriage has changed over the years. How would you describe yourself when you first married—and how has that girl changed over the years? And what about your husband? In what significant ways has he changed? How has the need for forgiveness inside your marriage changed you? How has it changed your husband?

My thirty-one-year-old son told me recently that he couldn't remember his dad and me fighting when he was a child. He said he had no memory of our arguments. I laughed, telling him I was glad for it but that there were plenty of angry words between his dad and me. There were slammed doors. There were times one or the other of us left the house, got in the car, and drove off in a major huff to let off steam before finishing an argument.

While I remember what some of those big fights were about, I don't hold an account. And there are other fights where I can't even remember what we argued about—and there's a reason: I forgave Will. Real forgiveness lacks emotional memory. The details are all there, but the angry heart reaction isn't. That's grace. And it's exactly the kind of grace God offers each of us in our life with him. He knows the details, but he doesn't hold it over our heads. We're free. But there's even more

There is no
relationship
more intimate
and no relationship
that requires the
rawest authenticity
like that in a

marriage.

to grace than just forgiveness. There's also a sense of favor, an undeserved love and attention for the offending party.

I love the way author Max Lucado describes it. He writes, "The difference between mercy and grace? Mercy gave the Prodigal Son a second chance. Grace gave him a feast."* Yeah, let that one sink in a minute. If you want grace in your marriage, it's not enough to just forgive. And it's not enough to just forget. If we're going to have a marriage characterized by grace, it's going to take that occasional feast. And that goes both ways.

But since I'm not writing to your husband and we can't force him to give you a feast, let's just think on this question: What would it look like to hold a feast in your husband's honor? To set aside the stuff that gets in between the two of you and "come to terms with this once and for all and then walk beside him as heirs together of the grace of life?"**

---

*   Max Lucado (@MaxLucado), "The difference between mercy and grace?" Twitter, January 17, 2011, 7:19 a.m., https://twitter.com/maxlucado/status/27022300356284416?lang=en
** Elisabeth Elliot, *Let Me Be a Woman* (Carol Stream, IL: Tyndale House, 1976), 82.

For me, it means being tender and kind. It means thinking of Will's needs above my own. That's an awful lot of everyday energy. But this feast of grace in my marriage also requires something else. It requires faith. The kind of faith that feels small and vulnerable and sometimes a little frightening. The kind of faith in God that believes God will always look out for me even as I'm looking out for someone else. That kind of faith. I need faith that God will complete the work he began in my husband even as he completes the work he began in me. The feast of grace means surrendering to that truth even when it feels like God is always working to grow me but not my husband. Can you relate?

Many of the young women I mentor feel the same way. They see (and feel) the hard work God is doing in their lives but don't always see the work God is doing in their husbands' lives. So it looks like all the feast-making is for Adam but not for Eve. So Eve sometimes likes to take things in her own hands and preempts God by giving Adam a few directions on how to be a good husband. She offers instructions on what it looks like to be a godly man. Of course, the only problem with that is Eve isn't a man, isn't a husband, and isn't the Teacher.

The faith required for the feast is a surrender to God's omniscience as a teacher and an able leader. It's ultimately submission to God. So faith comes by uttering a prayer like this: Thank you, God, for growing my husband into the man he needs to be to lead this family. I pray that you'll help me to love him, encourage him, and serve him in any way I am able. Help me to make a feast of grace for him by forgiving him and honoring him. Amen.

Maybe today is the day you tell your husband you'd marry him all over again. Because by saying Yes to him again, you're speaking grace over him and your marriage. Write a letter to your husband and tell him you say Yes.

CHAPTER SEVEN

Grace for
Mothers

As a mother, you have the opportunity to form your home and family life in such a way that God's reality comes alive to your children each day.

—SALLY CLARKSON

It's five a.m., Saturday morning. I woke early to write, knowing the only time I will put pen to paper is right now in the quiet. Just the cat curled up at my feet, vintage diner mug full of strong, black coffee, and my Moleskine notebook. I put this time aside early because I know the rest of the day I will gladly surrender with passionate interest to the people staying in my home.

Emily and Kenton are living in the treehouse (our

garage apartment) for the month while they wait on their housing situation to open up in Dripping Springs, just twenty miles west of our home. And Sara and Davey came in for a friend's wedding. It was complete and glorious bedlam yesterday when sisters, Emily and Sara, saw each other for the first time in over a month. All kinds of squealing and hugging and picture-taking.

My life feels fullest when my children are around me. I think that's the heart of most mothers I know. And while my husband and I have established and enjoy our empty-nest home, when our kids come flooding back to us, our full attention falls on them. Because there's nothing like the joy of having grown children who want to spend time with you. It speaks to the unconditional love they have for you, which is truly grace.

Because who, besides your husband, sees your journey and your real self in all totality, like your children? Who sees you missing the mark, making mistakes, and sometimes living a contradiction like your children do? Your family truly sees you inside out.

When my kids were little, I had big dreams of being a perfect mother. But the truth is, at that early stage, I

was in the middle of God doing some really deep healing work in my life over the things that happened in my
childhood that caused me to be fearful. I am so grateful
God healed me. But I'm even more thankful that God
helped me mother my kids into a healthy relationship
with him in spite of my weakness.

A couple months back on the Dear Daughters pod-
cast, I interviewed Emily and I asked her what she
would have loved to say to me when she was twelve
years old. Surprised at the question, she sat silent for a
minute and then she gently said, "I wish I could have
told you not to be afraid. That everything was going
to be okay."

I was stunned into tears because that's not what I
was expecting to hear. As a parent, I know that's what
a mother should say to a child, not vice versa. But that's
where I was in my journey for twelve-year-old Emily.
Still getting a ton of healing over things that happened
to me as a child.

Through tears I said back to her, "Oh, Emily, I am
so sorry. I wish I could have been more whole for you,
but we're not put together, we're being put together." It
was a humbling moment and a reminder for me that, no

There's nothing like
the joy of having
grown children who
want to spend time with
you. It speaks to
the unconditional love
they have for you,
which is

truly grace.

matter where I am in my journey with my people, I am in still process with God as he continues to heal, restore, repair, and make new.

I love my children so much. I wish I could have presented them with a perfect mother at every age in their lives. A woman who was never selfish, fearful, or wrong. Instead they got the real me: a woman on a journey with God, growing into wisdom and wholeness.

I bet you feel the same. You want to be the best mother. One who never makes mistakes, never fails, and always presents the most accurate picture of God's love in their lives. Wouldn't that be wonderful? To be the perfect role model? There's a real longing there, to be who God wants us to be for our people.

In my conversations with young women, I have found that longing to be a perfect mother is especially strong for women who didn't have a good relationship with their own mothers. They seem to possess a fierce desire to right the wrong they endured as children by being the perfect mother. Or their picture of perfect.

I think of Amy, mama to two young ones, who told me her workaholic mother was always busy and emotionally distant when she raised her. As a result,

Amy is a stay-at-home mom who continually makes ever-present decisions to "be" with her children. But she still worries it's not enough somehow and that her children will feel an absence. Because Amy didn't experience closeness with her mother, she feels she doesn't know how to be close to her children, even though she's trying as hard as she can. She feels restless and inadequate.

And then there's Clare, mama to one young son. Clare's mother suffered from undiagnosed bipolar disorder much of Clare's childhood. Because of her mother's illness, Clare's childhood was a continual emotional rollercoaster propelled by the ups and downs of her mom's manic-depressive episodes. Clare has a deep mother wound and constantly worries the lack of mothering she received impacts her ability to adequately parent her own son.

Both women still grieve their own mothers' inability to give them what they needed when they were young. Both wish for a different, and healthier, relationship with their mothers currently. The losses from their own childhoods bleed into the parenting of their own children. And they know it, so it then creates a cycle of sadness, despair, and eventual resentment.

When I talk with Amy and Clare and listen to their stories, I can hear the ache in their voices. Their suffering is ever-present. Sometimes in moments of great transparency, I hear them worry aloud if they'll somehow be just like their own mothers—present but absent. It's a battle for them to overcome all the tension and the bitterness.

These conversations point to the fact that everyone has mother wounds. Because no mother is perfect. So every child at some point and time must be willing to forgive her mother for all the things. And there are so many things.

In my situation with Emily, I would never have known that I needed to apologize to her twelve-year-old self for being a fearful mom had I not asked the question in our interview. Looking back, I am grateful she felt safe enough with me now to uncover her truth. What grace! And not only that, my apology modeled for her what a wise mother does in a relationship with a child. It's my prayer she will carry the experience into her own mothering when she has children someday. The result is that the honesty between us created even deeper connection, and that's what I'm after as a mother.

If you could write a letter to your mother, what would you say? How does what you would say to your mom impact how you're mothering your own children? This is the kind of exercise that could really help you understand any mother wounds you have and how they have bled into your current parenting. I also think it's important to write this out because, if you're like most young women I talk to, you'll probably need to forgive your mother. Until you forgive your own mother for the something or other she did to you in your life, you'll never fully be the grace you want to be to your children. Forgiveness unlocks all kinds of grace. I encourage you to do the work regardless of how difficult it may seem.

And then, what about this? If you could write a letter to your children, what would you say? Would you tell them about how you want to mother well but don't always know how? Would you ask them to forgive you for the things you did or didn't do? Would you tell them about your hopes for their lives and your relationship?

Would you give them a peek at your tender, sometimes fragile mama heart? That could create all kinds of wonder between you two.

I'll never forget when my son, Will III, went off to college. I had this ginormous revelation about all the potential ways I could have failed him as a mother, and so I sat down and wrote him a long email, apologizing for the ways I might have disappointed him the last eighteen years of his life. A couple hours after I sent the letter, he called me and said, "Mom … are you okay? Because I'm okay. I mean, thank you for this letter but you were a good mom to me." I bawled and then we laughed. That letter was good for both of us.

You will never be the mother you want to be to your children without grace towards the imperfections—those of your own and those of others. Letters are good medicine. Write one today.

And remember, God can heal the broken places in your life. He can do all kinds of miraculous things in your life and in your relationship.* He can make you the kind of mama you want to be for your kids. Regardless

---

*   Ephesians 3:20

of how you were mothered, he can give you the kind of relationship you crave with them. Surrender yourself to him.

And if you're a dear daughter with a mama-sized hole in your heart, I pray God's deepest comfort over all the heartache. I pray he himself will mother you. Amen.

CHAPTER EIGHT

Grace for

Insecurity

The beautiful part of my insecurity is that it keeps me running to a God who is the only way that I'm secure, known, and complete. I've decided it's what makes me who I am, and keeps me at the foot of the cross. And I'm okay with that thorn.

——CHRYSTAL EVANS HURST

When my husband and I got the call from my son, Will III, asking if we could watch our grandson, Caleb, so he and his wife, Amy, could take their first overnight getaway—the answer was a ginormous yes. There is nothing that fills my heart to overflowing like time with that precious baby boy. He is the happiest, most joyful baby I've ever met, and the idea of spending a full twenty-four hours with him delighted me. But I have to be honest; I also felt a twinge of uneasiness. After raising three children of my own, I never imagined that I'd experience any nervousness about whether I could actually handle the assignment of watching a baby overnight, especially my own grandson. But I did feel a mix of trepidation alongside the excitement.

When we got to their house, Amy gave me all the instructions along with his schedule, and then she said, "The only thing is, he's starting this thing where he wants to skip one of his naps. And then he gets exhausted and overtired. I'm afraid today might be one of those days." I assured her that Bear and Zuzu (those are our grandparent names) were up to the task and shooed them out the door to take a break and relax and enjoy.

We played with Caleb, fed him dinner, and then started his nighttime routine. Diaper changed, book read, bottle fed—but he wouldn't close his eyes. Instead his big blue eyes were locked on mine. Occasionally, he tried to sit up or pull off the bottle and look around. The one time I went to put him in his crib, he cried and cried big alligator tears. Bedtime just wasn't happening. So I called Will in to help. He walked Caleb around, coaxing him to settle down and close his eyes. Slowly but surely, Caleb got more and more tired. Finally, Will handed him back to me and I gave him the bottle once more—and this time, the minute he took the milk his eyes drooped and closed. I slowly made my way to his room and laid him down. He lifted his big blue eyes to mine once more, then finally they closed, and he slipped off to sleep.

I tiptoed out of his room and when I did, I remembered something I'd heard a long time ago about sleep. It's the most vulnerable thing a person can do. Think about it. When you fall asleep at night, you're wholly and completely defenseless. Vulnerable to anything. It's quite amazing that God made us that way—to need something that makes us so helpless. But all creation needs sleep. And so all creation sleeps, letting its guard down and opening up to rest.

I think that's an important thing to note. This idea that God requires complete physical vulnerability every twelve or so hours. Our bodies need it, even crave it. And I think our souls need and crave it, too. To have the

We need
to be able to
process the whole
of our stories to
have healthy
hearts.

space to let our guard down. I think that's why so many dear daughters want to talk to me about their lives. Because one of the ways we experience that vulnerability is by telling our stories, and the good and bad in them. We need to be able to process the whole of our stories to have healthy hearts. I have found that writing letters to your younger self is one way to get at that soulish kind of health.

We're more than halfway through this, you and me. And I'm wondering if you've been answering the questions that come up in the chapters. I'm curious if you're actually putting pen to paper and doing the soul work.

When I mentor women and ask questions, sometimes they're reluctant to answer honestly. Sometimes they're so used to protecting themselves and their stories, they don't want or maybe even know how to be real and honest about the condition of their hearts.

So often, I offer to go first. I ask a probing question and then I answer it—modeling what it looks like to be vulnerable. And I'm actually going to do that with you right now by writing an extended letter to my younger self during the most fragile time in my life.

I'm going to write it all out here for you to read and

then, prayerfully, get a glimpse of what it really looks like to give grace in the deepest places. Those spaces in your life that need God and his grace the most.

To date, my deepest well of insecurity over the nature of God and our relationship was when I was a young mama about twenty-four years old. Of course I didn't realize this, but you live life forward and you understand it backward. Looking back at that young woman I would have written this.

Dear twenty-four-year-old Susie,

Hi little mama.

There you are with your precious boy and husband by your side, plus a church he's pastoring. Well, you've really got all you ever wished and hoped for. And it's beautiful. But it's also so much more work than you ever dreamed, right?

Taking care of your baby plus being a wife … even better, being a pastor's wife. And oh yeah, throw finishing school into the mix. Taking a full load in one year just so you can graduate. It's a lot. But you know what? You'll learn after a couple decades, it's typical Susie style to say yes, and then

*jump in big time. So I want to give you a preview
of some of those jumps you'll take.*

*In a couple years, you and Will actually start
a church in Austin from nothing. No income, no
insurance. He might have kind of pushed you off the
ledge on that one. But you'll love it. And so will he.
You jumped.*

*You'll create and start a theater program at
a Christian school and teach there ten years. No
matter that you don't have a theater or teaching
degree. You just jump.*

*You become an author and write books. Seven
of them. I know! Big God dream right there. It
happened.*

*You end up on the radio on a morning show.
I know it sounds like a joke. Cause like, no
experience, right? You jump anyway, and it's
really good.*

*And this one: remember when you rode horses as
a kid, and you dreamed one day to own one? That
happened. And you end up riding horses for literally
decades. Isn't that the loveliest thing?*

You do all kinds of crazy wonderful things.

But right now, you're not sure who you're supposed to be just yet, and you're still learning a lot about marriage, ministry, and being a mother to baby Will. You're learning about juggling all those things. And that's okay. It's all okay. Because you have lots of time.

But can we talk for a minute about what you're hiding in your heart? What's tucked down there so deep that you don't talk about it to anyone, even your husband?

You're scared. Frightened that something awful is going to happen … again. Like it did when you were a fourteen-year-old sitting in your English class completely vulnerable, just talking and laughing with friends. And then a fellow student, who was also your neighbor two doors up, came in with a rifle. Stood three feet from your teacher, pointed the gun at his chest, and shot him right there in front of your eyes. Body hit the floor. Blood under his head. Your teacher lay dying. It was brutal. Horrific. Tragic.

And it changed your life. You walked into school

that day worried about how your hair looked and wondering if your boyfriend was going to walk you home from school.

You walked out of school that day escorted by police officers, shielding you and your classmates from news crews with cameras. When your teacher died, a piece of you died, too. Susie, I'm so sorry you had to see that. Truly. It was scary and horrible, and it made you afraid.

The thing is, even though you're ten years removed now at twenty-four, all the fear generated by the murder is still sitting in your heart. And it's spiraled into dread of anything bad happening. To anybody you love. And now especially ... you're terrified that something's going to happen to that precious little baby boy. And the very thought of that literally unravels your heart. And has you scrambling to control anything and everything.

It started with your pregnancy, remember? You pored over that big ole book, What to Expect When You're Expecting, *and followed the rules religiously. You read everything you could to protect the health of your unborn baby. And made that big important list of no-no's. No sodium nitrate. No sulfites. No caffeine. Oh, and no highlighting your hair. Uh-uh. It might seep into your scalp and hurt the baby. You did all the right things for a healthy pregnancy.*

Of course, when the big day finally came, nothing went as planned. Your hopes for an epidural-free delivery like your sister's turned into nine hours of labor and then an emergency C-section. That was certainly a surprise. You got through it like a champ though. And oh gracious it was worth it because oh, that baby boy.

But do you remember how after he was born you still kept trying to control everything? How you felt if you could manage his physical world, you could ensure his safety?

I mean some of it was just good common sense. Like breastfeeding over the bottle. But some of it was way over the top, fueled by that deep fear that infected your life. Like when Will's college buddies drove in from out of town to see the baby ... and at the last minute you were freaking out so bad that you didn't let them inside because you were worried they might have germs or something that would hurt him. So you had them stand on the back patio and look at the baby through the window, kind of like you and the baby lived in a bubble-wrapped world. I know in your mind you were being a good mother. But if you fast-forward some years you'll see how this was all a little strange and how the behavior was evidence of a fear stronghold. You'll see that this was not only overkill but also probably made Will's friends think he married a weirdo.

It really did start for you that day in eighth grade. Because, let's be honest, it seems like God turned his back on you. Or maybe he was just too busy taking care of more important things on the other side of the world than protecting you. And now you're afraid God might be the same way with your baby boy. Too busy to take note and take care.

Here's this:

Yes, you love God desperately.

But you don't trust him with yourself or your baby boy.

And it's created a chasm in your soul.

On the outside, you have it all together.

But on the inside, you're suffering, silently. Praying desperately for God to keep the world a safe place but knowing it's not. Praying for protection over how completely defenseless you feel. Because this thing that happened is the crux of your struggle to have a real faith in God. It is a desperate struggle for you.

While this is sounding kind of bleak, I want to tell you that you do overcome it by God's grace and strength. Because God didn't forget you, Susie. And there's a lot of good news. Let me encourage you with a little of it.

In about a year, you're going to get pregnant again, and you're going to have a little girl and name her Emily. Oh joy! A boy and a girl. Now, Emily will be terrifically strong-willed. And she will wear you out. And you will try to bubble-wrap your world again, but it won't work because she won't let it. And that's a good thing. Her high spirits are a part of your redemptive story. So don't be too hard on her.

Oh and then this … three years after Emily, there's Sara. And she will be the easiest child, the angel baby of life.

Another thing—really soon you're going to meet an older woman named Jane and she's going to walk through a Bible study with you and your friends. It really doesn't matter that you don't finish the study. The main thing is … you pray a dangerous prayer. You want to hear it? It's not super fancy. Here goes. You pray: "God, if there's anything you need to heal in me … will you heal it?" That's what you pray. You won't have even known you needed healing, but you'll jump, and God will catch you big time to start healing you from all fear hidden deep. He loves you so much.

In that healing, you'll slowly discover that control is just a coping mechanism. To deal with the pain. And you'll come to understand hyper-control doesn't keep bad things from happening in the future. But it does extinguish the joy of the present. And joy is what you're after. That free-spirited joy you had as a little girl.

And oh this … you get back your joy in God

and then some. And guess who gets a real kick out of it? Your boy. Your son. Matter of fact, at Sara's wedding (YES! They all get married to the most wonderful people!!) he says, "Mom, you are just on complete joy overload, spinning around."

And his sweet wife, Amy, you know what she says? She says, "Suz, you're the only person I know who is aging backwards."

So Susie, I can tell you this from all my fifty-five years of experience: When you are bound up in anxiety, you'll miss the daily wonder. Like how God has filled the world to the brim with curious beauty. How he whispers to the sun and it rises.

Let him whisper to you, too.

I want you to be open to your one beautiful life.
Because you only get one, right?
So walk forward into the unexpected, pain and all.
Walk forward in faith, though at times limping,
knowing that God is still there for you.

Take tiny, brave steps forward today. No thinking about tomorrow's problems or next week's issues. Just for today, think only on today.

And as you practice that one thing, for just today, know you are actively loving and trusting God. And all you can really ever do is love God today. In this one moment, loving and trusting, pushing aside fear and worry.

And just as the sun surrenders daily to God's hand, I'm praying you find that small space to surrender your heart to God, too.

Know this: I love you. I really do. I love your strength and I love your weakness, too. Because that's the place God's grace shines most brightly through you.

> *Love,*
> *Your fifty-five-year-old self*

CHAPTER NINE

Grace for
the Seasons

There comes a time when the things that
were undoubtedly good and right in the past
must be left behind, for there is always the danger
that they might hinder us from moving forward
and connecting with the one necessary thing,
Christ himself.

—ESTHER DE WAAL

Our little black tuxedo cat, Madeleine, always knows when someone in our family is packing up and leaving our house. And if she likes you, she'll crawl up in your suitcase, curl up in a ball, and go to sleep. We're never sure if this is her way to signal that she'd like to come along or if it's silent protest to your leaving. That's what she did for Sara, our youngest (and Madeleine's favorite), when Sara packed before leaving for college. Meanwhile, all I could think to do while watching our baby pack to fly out into the world was to make banana muffins. Maybe I was channeling my angst into baking. Many times, those same muffins were the very thing I made to entice Sara back home when she was away at a friend's house for the weekend. It always worked before; but even though I knew it wouldn't work now, that's how my mama heart instructed me to deal with the discomfort. I wanted her to stay home forever.

Forget the fact that she was nineteen years old and plenty old enough to pack up and head just seven miles west of our home to the campus of the University of Texas in Austin. Forget that. Because the cat and I knew we were going to miss her smiling face something awful. I handled it like any mother would. I gave her lots of last-minute advice and whipped up her favorite breakfast foods. Maybe I thought those warm muffins sitting on the kitchen counter would make her change her mind and keep living at home. I hoped she'd never leave. Because children should never leave home. But the end of a beautiful season was over. Sara was graduating to the next big step in her life and forcing me into my next season, too.

Transitions are tough. Especially when they involve my children. I remember when our oldest, Will III, went to kindergarten, I was the mama sobbing desperately in the hallway. My husband literally had to help me walk out of the school building that day. When he eventually went to college, my husband insisted my son and I say our goodbyes outside under a tree instead of in the dorm room. Maybe he was trying to save our son the embarrassment because he remembered my past breakdown, or maybe to make it easier on me. Either way I found myself alone under a tree at Baylor University crying my eyes out as my husband walked Will III back into his dorm to say goodbye.

The problem with the end of a season is that every time you face one, it means something must die. It might be a role, a job, or a life stage. Inside our lives, there is a constant cycle of things coming to life and then dying, much like what we see in nature season to season. Spring

If you think
you might be in a
transitional season
or if there's a little
emotional tug at
your soul,
I want to suggest
you ask God honest
questions about
what's going on.

brings all kinds of life, then give it a half year and it's as though winter takes it all away.

This last spring, it was all glorious in my front yard. First the bluebonnets, next Indian blankets, and then Indian paintbrushes. After that the purple bee balm took a turn. My dad calls it horsemint. Either way, it came in tall, purple, and profuse—covering the entire wild-flower field. Then finally, the black-eyed Susans popped up in the middle of it all with bright yellow petals and black center cone, so rich in contrast against the sea of soft purple bee balm. It was gorgeous. I loved it and have a billion pictures to prove it. Like a visual symphony.

Then in winter, it's quiet out in the yard. It looks like everything's lost; but of course, I know from watching it over and over—those flowers will show up again. The seeds are sleeping; transformation is taking place even if it looks like nothing is happening at all.

In our lives, it can feel much different and more difficult. So often I want to hang on to a season I love, like the one of mothering children at home. And so when it's time for a goodbye, the grief therein takes me by surprise. It's just so hard to let go. Is that how the seasonal changes of life impact you, too?

What season of life are you in? Are you loving your one beautiful life right now? Or are you in the middle of a season of goodbyes that makes you feel like you just can't love your life at all? Is there grief piled up in your life? How are the goodbyes for you? Is it hard to let go of the things you love, like your job or a friendship or even your children?

Recently I had a conversation with a dear daughter in her early forties who is entering a season of change in her life. She has one son in college and two daughters in high school. As we talked, I asked her questions. We talked around a lot of things when finally, I asked, "What would you say your greatest angst is at this time?" Tears popped to her eyes and she said, "Everything's changing, and I don't know what to do."

I appreciated her honesty. And her tears were telling. A major season of life was moving in on her, but that's not what was making her sad. It was the reality behind the seasonal change that made her feel emotional. With one child at college and her girls coming up right behind, she knows it's time to count the days and treasure up all those mama moments. She was pre-grieving what she knows is coming up.

When I first started meeting with my spiritual director, Janet, I told her nearly the same thing. Sara, the baby of the family, was six months married and I stumbled into Janet's house with my heart ragged and torn apart for all the grief. But I didn't know it because I was also so joyful over her marriage. Matter of fact, I was appreciative and joyful about all three of my kids' marriages. So it didn't make sense that I should feel sad over something I hoped for, prayed toward, and eventually saw come to fruition. Janet was the one to help me see that I was saying a hard, long goodbye to a beautiful time in my life, that of being a mother responsible for the care of children living at home.

If you think you might be in transitional season or if there's a little emotional tug at your soul, I want to suggest you ask God honest questions about what's going on. Is there a chance your heart is telling you that there's a goodbye you might be avoiding? That maybe there's some grief rising up? Remember, tears are always telling.

Though you might feel like running (or just mindlessly making banana muffins) or taking a cue from Madeleine and cramming yourself into someone's suitcase, I encourage you to befriend the feelings welling up in your heart. Let them speak. Write things down. Answer these questions: What season of my life is changing? How is that making me sad? What am I grieving? Answer the questions without censoring yourself.

After you identify exactly what is going on in your heart and your life, I want to suggest that you write a goodbye letter. Yep. Write a letter to whomever you are saying goodbye to in this season of your life. You don't need to send it. This might be just for you. Or you could write it and share it. Either way, getting your words down on paper will help you understand what makes this goodbye mean so much.

In it, you can list the losses you're feeling completely free of judgment. Don't be afraid of the chaos you may be feeling. Because underneath it all, that's often where transformation happens. Real abundance is being present to all of life. The highs and the lows. The good times and the grief. Living an abundant life is about being awake to all life has to offer.

I told you so much about my transitions with Will III that I feel like sharing an open letter I wrote him on the morning he got married, which if you haven't experienced yet—you'll come to realize—it's really the final mothering goodbye. I'm sharing this because, unlike when Will was younger, this goodbye did not come as a surprise. I didn't feel ambushed, as I often did at other moments as he grew up. I walked into his wedding awake in life, present to the abundance even though it was painful. Here's the letter I wrote to my son on the day of his wedding.

Dear Will,

Today you're getting married to this beautiful girl named Amy … I can hardly believe it's true. And I'm sitting here in my hotel room with this sense that I need to be doing something, anything. Because isn't that just like a mother? Always busy for her children?

But I'm realizing, it's all done. This big, beautiful job of mothering you. C-o-m-p-l-e-t-e. It's time to let go. It's time to let another woman know you and love you in a way that goes much deeper than a mother's love. That's kind of hard to say. But it's true.

So it's time for me to sit still and quiet. To stop working and rest. And if I'm honest ... to listen to Sufjan Stevens's "Holy, Holy, Holy" one more time while I sip my coffee and let myself cry and cry and cry.

I never thought I'd rest from mothering. Never thought I'd stop worrying over you. Thinking of you. But this morning I am joyful in realizing today is the day. And I will rejoice.

Today is the day to rejoice in knowing you are a man who loves Jesus deeply, tenderly, tenaciously. A man who walked out the first twenty-six years of his life close to Christ and often apart from the crowd. Because you held the hope that this day would come. And it would be worth the wait.

Today is the day to rejoice in knowing my prayers (and your dad's) were answered.

And her name is Amy.

In this deep open space of rest, I want to make some promises to you and Amy. And I want to commit to new prayers based on God's words.

I will give them a heart to know me,
that I am the LORD. Jeremiah 24:7

I will pray that you and Amy will have one heart. You and Amy, one heart. Not me and Dad and you and Amy … but you and Amy. And I pray that your dad and I would be gracious in understanding and accepting your life plans. Even if it doesn't involve living in Austin.

If God is for us, who can be against us? He who did not spare his own Son but gave him up for us all, how will he not also with him graciously give us all things? Romans 8:31-32

I pray that you and Amy would understand and feel God's deep support. That in hard times you would cling to the truth that God is for you. And I want you to know your dad and I are for you. And just like God, there is nothing we wouldn't give up for you. Nothing we wouldn't sacrifice to support your marriage.

Will. I love you. And I love Amy.
And I rejoice.

Mom

Just reading that letter I wrote seven years ago now makes me grateful. My heart is to be a woman who is good with goodbye. Don't you want to be good with goodbye, too? Because there are so many we'll need to say. And the truth is, because of God, abundance waits on the other side of every season.

As spring gives way to summer and then fall—season to season in your life—and things are cleared away, what remains there? Who remains there, the same year after year? I hope you see God. Because the loneliness we all seek to fill after every goodbye is only found in him. He is the wholeness our hearts seek. And he is our comfort.

CHAPTER TEN

Grace for

Mentors

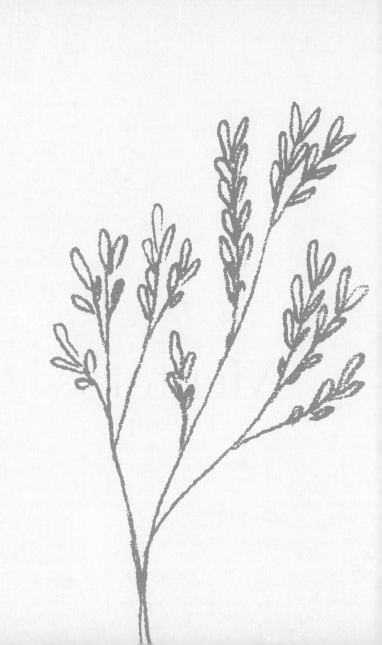

... when we tell the truth about our lives—the broken parts, the secret parts, the beautiful parts— then the Gospel comes to life, an actual story about redemption, instead of abstraction and theory and things you learn in Sunday School.

—SHAUNA NIEQUIST

My passion for mentoring started in the kitchen. I remember standing across from my children and their friends, making one meal after another to feed hungry high schoolers. They would come en masse on late nights, and I'd make them my favorite homemade margherita pizza recipe. While I stood there kneading out the dough, I got to take part in the most beautiful conversations.

My kids' friends knew when they came into my home, I was going to ask them questions about God and life. I loved hearing about what God was doing in their lives. Often, they would ask me questions, too, and I'd tell them about the times God showed up in my life. In the course of the conversation, I was able to deeply encourage these kids while I stood there making pizza or peanut butter and jelly sandwiches and sliding them across the counter.

For me, mentoring was born out of mothering. I never thought of myself as a mentor, and I'm grateful because it actually might have intimidated me. But I did think of myself more as another mother who had an interest in talking about spiritual things. Often, they told me that they'd never had a conversation about deep things of God in their lives with an adult before, but they liked it. They started calling me Mama Suz and that's how these girls became my dear daughters. It was organic, natural. I was simply answering a call by leaning into the parts of me I already felt confident in: the mothering parts, the encouraging parts, the parts that liked feeding people and making them feel at home.

Over the last decade as I have embraced my age (I'm fifty-five years old) and felt more comfortable in my role as a mentor, I have come to understand e-v-e-r-y-b-o-d-y needs a spiritual mama. You need a spiritual mama; I need a spiritual mama. We all need women just a few steps ahead who are willing to lend wisdom and care.

Someone who will ask thoughtful questions. Someone who will listen. And maybe even make you a margherita pizza or a peanut butter and jelly sandwich and slide it across the counter. To help you see your life, and to remind you that God is present. And every little thing is going to be okay. Wouldn't that be lovely?

But the sad truth is the more women I mentor, the more I'm aware that so many women don't have spiritual mamas. Even more of a heartbreak is the fact that many of those very women have difficult relationships with their own mothers, which creates an even deeper void. Lots of dear daughters I talked with say that their mothers are emotionally distant or distracted by a big career or even a gut-wrenching divorce. Many are saddened because they feel their own mothers are immature relationally or spiritually and unable to be the voice of wisdom in their lives. There are so many dear daughters in the world. The world needs more spiritual mamas. Even those of us with the best and most capable mothers still need someone outside of ourselves to remind us of what God thinks about us and how he might be working. What we need are more spiritual mamas.

With 50 percent of the female population forty-five years old and above, you would think we would have an army of spiritual mamas in the world. But we don't. And I think it's because the very women who would make excellent mentors don't think they're qualified. And they don't understand how easy it is to be one.

Good mentoring is born, in part, out of what you already do well. It's not usually about going out to find someone, but living into your strengths and giftings, and being open to the people whom God draws to you. Just like what happened with me.

It's also born in understanding that you have what it takes—and you don't have to have it all together. Do you worry you're underqualified? You look over your life and think you've made such a mess of it that no one could possibly think of you as a mentor. Or maybe you feel you're steady and faithful but awfully boring. That you lack the passion and pizzazz of women you see in church or online leading others spiritually.

Well, I have some good news for you. The wisdom of a good mentor/spiritual mama is earned in two ways. One, by doing the right thing in life and winning the reward. Second, by doing the wrong thing in life and suffering the consequences. Chances are you've had both of those types of learning experiences. I know I sure have.

I think most of my dear daughters would say that they learn most from me when I share how I failed God or my people in some way and how God loved and cared for me, nonetheless. When I share those stories (versus the ones in which I did everything right), they feel encouraged and understood. Because we're all needy children of God in the big story, right?

It's about being vulnerable, about how God is working to transform us in our own lives. We put our egos on the shelf and share how God is glorious even when we are far less than glorious. About how God can make something beautiful of our lives even in the dark and lonely places. We share our stories, the whole of them,

Good mentoring
is born, in part,
out of what you already
do well. It's not usually
about going out to find
someone, but living into
your strengths and
giftings, and being open
to the people whom
God draws to you.

not just the prettied-up parts. That's when we are the best kind of spiritual mamas, with authenticity shining inside out.

A couple months back, I was invited by my friend Amy Hannon to come to Springdale, Arkansas. She owns a kitchen boutique called Euna Mae's and she kindly offered to celebrate my book *Dear Daughters* with a book signing and dessert party.

About forty women gathered in the kitchen area of her lovely store and I shared with them much of what I have shared with you here about how I came to be a mentor, how the world needs more spiritual mamas, and how spiritual mamas are just regular people in need of a big God.

After sharing my story, I asked the women if they had any questions. A forty-something woman stood up and walked bravely to the microphone. She shared that one of her biggest fears in mentoring and being a spiritual mama was that she felt she had failed a mentee. She said in one particular relationship, she made the mistake of continuing to mentor even though she was running out of steam spiritually. She said she was so burned out spiritually, she couldn't fulfill her role as a mentor. And because of this, she worried she would duplicate the situation again.

She teared up while she was talking, feeling as though she was somehow a big disappointment. I held her arm and looked her in the eyes and said, "What you described—this need to take a break—is normal. We all need to take a break sometimes. And what you lived before that girl is the real life of every believer. Not an Instagram picture of a coffee mug, a Bible, and a candle, but a real life in need of Jesus." And then I asked her if she had a mentor while she was mentoring. She said no. And I encouraged her to find a mentor so that she had someone looking out for the health of her soul.

What about you? Are you running out of steam spiritually? Are you feeling overwhelmed? Is there a chance you are taking care of everyone else and not yourself? Always leading others, leaving nothing for yourself? I get it. It's easy to give and give until you feel like you're completely spent.

Can I have a minute, just you and me? And can I speak to the weariness you're wearing? This letter is just for you.

Oh hey you. How are you? No I mean, really … how are you doing?

I see you out there living your life for Jesus and serving him. Your passion is evident. But I also see behind that tired smile a wish for a little rest. And a desire that someone was looking out for you the way you're always looking out for others. Maybe you have a spiritual mama speaking alongside you in your life—I sure hope so. But if you don't, I'm going to step in and say some things.

No wonder you're tired. You've been caring for people for so long now. I can see how you're worn thin, so close to not having anything to give. It doesn't mean you're failing. Everybody who loves God feels like that sometimes. And that's actually when you have the chance to step into some real grace, the kind you've been extending to the people who look up to you.

It's more than okay to be the kind of spiritual mama who says, "I love God and I love you, but I need some time for me." Take the time you need to regroup. Get yourself some space. Find the rest that really changes how you feel about your life and the people you're trying to serve.

It's what a wise mama does, you know? Remember when your own kids were little, how you would sneak off to find a minute to take a breath and settle your heart? Your little ones were just fine without you for a minute or two. And then remember when you started having a sitter watch them? How you handed them off to a trusted someone so that you could do something mindless and wonderful like stroll the aisles at Target or have lunch with a friend? Those babies were just fine without you.

In the same way, you need to know that the women under your influence are going to be fine without you. Others will rise up, and of course, God will take care. He's always taking care.

Will you let him take care of you, too? Faithfulness is not about always working hard. Sometimes it's about stepping away and taking a break. Sometimes it's about being willing to disappoint others for the sake of wholeness with God. Jesus went away. He disappointed people. He left literal crowds of people who were calling out his name with very real problems. Permission to act like Jesus and step away from the crowd calling your name. If Jesus needed it, you need it, too.

A dear daughter needs to see a spiritual mama living a life of wholeheartedness before God and the people who need her. When you are the realest you—the one who is fragile and tender and needs respite—that's when they see they can be human, too. That's when they start to understand what it means to live a life with God and for him but not be used up by serving him. And isn't that the real grace? We don't have to work for love or acceptance or belonging. We just receive it—hands up, head bowed, heart expectant.

Your dear daughters will bless your name seeing you live a life of neediness before God. So go ahead and be needy for rest and time away. Be needy and take care of yourself. And may I suggest one of the first things you should do with your time away? Find someone to take care of you.

You need a spiritual mama, too. It's important for you no matter your age. You need someone

*whose whole agenda is for you and your
relationship with God. To see where your life is
spiritually. To ask you questions and let some holy
silence sink into the spaces where you don't have
answers yet. Wouldn't that be lovely? Will you look
for her until you find her?*

*Now, something to bring you comfort in the
meanwhile. Every little thing starts and ends with
Jesus. It says so in the book of Ephesians.* So rest
and know that every little thing will be okay. Do
the things that make you smile today. Do the things
that connect you to the important people in your life
who fuel and restore you. Give yourself permission
to take time for yourself. And when you lay your
head on the pillow tonight, know that you're
enough. More than enough, and you are loved by
the God who made you, and the dear daughters
in your life, and the whole big, wide world. And
remember, it's all going to be okay.*

I love you.

---

*   Ephesians 1:10

CHAPTER ELEVEN

Live Your One Beautiful Life

We have the idea that God is going to do some
exceptional thing, that He is preparing and fitting
us for some extraordinary thing by and bye, but as
we go on in grace, we find that God is glorifying
Himself here and now, in the present minute.
If we have God's say-so behind us, the most
amazing strength comes, and we learn to sing
in the ordinary days and ways.

—OSWALD CHAMBERS

The meal was delicious. Grilled pork tenderloin with
cucumber chutney, cheese grits, and slow-cooked green
beans. You can be sure I asked Rebecca to share her
recipes with me because everything she served us that
summer night was just delicious. And I'm not sure if the
Huffmans were expecting an impromptu rave after the
peach cobbler was served, but you'd never guess they

didn't do it with every family they invited to their house for supper.

The meal was fabulous, the entertainment raucous, but it was the conversation around the table that really impressed me. While it might seem like I posed a question that was a little too serious for the mood described, it turned out to elicit such heartfelt responses that I'd like to ask you, too. Okay, here goes: If you only had one year to live, what would you do with your life?

I know. A tad morose. But the thing is … the answers were beautiful. Rebecca said she'd write bunches of letters to her children and vacation with her sisters and her mama. Emily's friend Hillary (who was living with us that summer) said without hesitation that she'd drop out of college. My husband said he would hike till he died. Climb a mountain and die there. Like a real mountain man. I said I would quit work, write life instructions for my children, and make banana muffins for people. I also said I'd take more outdoor showers. But it was ten-year-old Ansley who brought me to tears. Ansley said she would get a starfish. She said if she knew she only had one year to live … she would get a starfish.

When I asked her why she wanted a starfish, she

said it was just because she loves the way they hang on things. Said she just always wanted a starfish. That's all. Just a starfish. *Isn't that beautiful?*

It's interesting how people get so singularly focused and how they can get at the very core of who they are when they're faced with thinking of life in terms of endings.

> What about you? If you knew you only had one
> year to live … what would you do?

The crazy truth is, you or I might only have a year to live. I mean, who knows? Only God alone. I'll tell you this for sure though, I don't want to be so absorbed in my worries that I miss all the wonder of the way God unfolds the mornings so soft and lovely across the Texas sky. Or too busy to sit on the floor and play with my grandson, Caleb, giving him my full attention. Or so distracted that I miss loving God in my here and now. I want to keep the end in mind so that I can live the middle of life fully present and aware of this gift from God. I want to live my one beautiful life.

What about you? Are you too feeling too busy to see

God loves
you right where you
are, and he's actively
working in your
life, in your unique
circumstances.

the gifts in your own life? Too distracted to observe the awe in your story? Or too caught up in all the right things to do for God that you miss his grace over your life?

The secret to living your one beautiful life is about thanking God *even though* things aren't exactly as you'd like them to be. It's about being tenacious and grateful in good times and bad times. That's the secret of living your one beautiful life. It's waking up and saying a prayer like this:

> I love you, God. I trust you.
> Thank you for my one beautiful life. Amen.

And then it's about walking through the day with God, having yielded to his plans for you even though you don't know what they look like. It's smiling at the future even when you don't know what the future holds.[*]

I recently attended the funeral of a man named Phil who died of cancer. Phil died early, too early, before any of his three sons married. Even before one of

---

[*] Proverbs 31:25 ESV

them graduated college. It was a breathtaking funeral because of the way Phil lived his life. Yes, about how he chose to live his life in those last few months with his friends and family. But also the way he lived his days all the years before his illness. I know this because of the words his best friend used to describe him. I know this because of the way his sons stood to eulogize him. And I saw it in the way his wife was steady and strong, grieving him but celebrating his beautiful life. His funeral was one of the best sermons I ever heard.

The Bible says it's better to spend your time at funerals than parties because we learn something from them.* The Bible also says when we number our days, we get a heart of wisdom.**

So what does it look like to number your days? As honestly as you can, answer this for me: How would you change your life if I told you that you only had months to live? Where would you spend your time and energy? Who would you spend it with? What kinds of things would you let slip off your plate? How would you start

---

*   Ecclesiastes 7:2 The Message

**   Psalm 90:12 ESV

treating differently the people you love the most? And how would you shift things in your relationship with God?

I think you would start numbering your days with wisdom. You would take God's truth to heart. You would reorganize your life in a way that emphasized who you really are at your core. You would embrace the opportunity to live the one beautiful life God has gifted you with right now. No more comparison. No more holding grudges, no wasting time on things you can't control. And no more missing the truth of who you are because of what God has done for you. No more skipping the grace.

Here are some truths about your life because of Jesus Christ. I want you to speak these aloud when you read them.

Through Jesus,
God's grace upon grace is all over my life.*
I am in God's family. I am a dearly loved daughter.**

---

* John 1:16

** John 1:12

*My cup overflows. His goodness
and love will pursue me always.**
*So I give thanks with a humble heart,
to the Giver of all good gifts.***

God loves you right where you are, and he's actively working in your life, in your unique circumstances. So no matter what season of life you're in, know this: God loves you. God sees you.

And your everyday story is the expression of his glory. And isn't that the most amazing grace?

That grace reaches down into the tiniest crevices of your life. Over all your days, in the smallest ways. How about you stand up inside of all that grace of God and embrace the glory of that truth in your life today?

Friend, put on that flower crown of grace, then walk around in it. Let God's love and light shine through you.

What would it take for you to go out and live your one beautiful life? If you only had one year to live, would

---

*   Psalm 23:5–6

**   James 1:17

you live today differently? Would you choose to be free and embrace the joy God offers?

> What would you do if you knew you only had
> one year to live?

Here's what I say: Take the grace that is yours. Then share that grace with others. Let go of offenses. Encourage the downhearted. Give God love. And let that love flood out to your neighbor. And, oh gracious please, love and accept yourself with a deep and wide kind of kindness.

Then get with your people. Sit at the table. Eat a delicious supper together. And by all means … dance.

Acknowledgments

—

Gratitude

Whitney Gossett: Thank you for championing my words, my passions, my ministry. I am delighted to do ministry with you. And I love knowing you like mysterious cats.

Esther and the Fedd team: Thank you for believing in and supporting me. I am grateful to work with women who love God and his Word—and who also love candles.

Karen Longino: Oh my gracious, what joy to know and work with you! Thank you for your tireless work to make this book a beautiful reality.

Chloe Hamaker: For patience, persistence, and all the pink questions. For being a comfort inside all types of creative chaos. I love you.

Bailey Greenlees: You jumped in. You wrangled an Enneagram 7's ministry dreams and you did it with such ease. I am grateful for the time we stood at my kitchen counter working plans. For the time we sat at the creek and calmed the creative storm. For Seven-Up and popcorn. For Tiny lunches. I love you, Bailey.

Jaime Cardinal: You are an answer to prayer. Thank you for listening to God and coming alongside just in the nick of time. There would be no *Grace Guide* without your thoughtful management of all the things. Here's to long Texas road trips and Twizzlers forever.

Dr. Andrew Forrester: Oh, yes, for all the words. For reading them and being gentle. For commas, colons, and quick turnarounds. You are my writing Sherpa.

Will Davis Jr.: For undamming the river and letting her go. For listening to the dreams and walking with me as we seek to serve God. I am grateful for you.

Will III, Emily, and Sara: For giving so much grace while I mothered you and for letting me grow in God alongside you. I love you. You are my joy.